T0300744

POLAR BEAR FUR ISN'T WHITE!

AND OTHER AMAZING FACTS

By Thea Feldman
Illustrated by Lee Cosgrove

Ready-to-Read

SIMON SPOTLIGHT

An imprint of Simon & Schuster Children's Publishing Division • New York London Toronto Sydney New Delhi
1230 Avenue of the Americas, New York, New York 10020 • This Simon Spotlight edition December 2020 • Text and illustrations
copyright © 2020 Simon & Schuster, Inc. Stock photos by iStock. All rights reserved, including the right of reproduction in whole or in part in
any form. SIMON SPOTLIGHT, READY-TO-READ, and colophon are registered trademarks of Simon & Schuster, Inc. For information about special
discounts for bulk purchases, please contact Simon & Schuster Special Sales at 1-866-506-1949 or business@simonandschuster.com. Manufactured
in the United States of America 1020 LAK • 10 9 8 7 6 5 4 3 2 1
Library of Congress Control Number 2020945222
ISBN 978-1-5344-7664-6 (hc)
ISBN 978-1-5344-7663-9 (pbk)
ISBN 978-1-5344-7665-3 (eBook)

GLOSSARY

absorb: to take in or soak up

blubber: a special kind of fat that ocean mammals have underneath their skin that helps keep them warm

carnivores: animals that eat mostly meat instead of plants

marine animals: animals that need to live near the ocean to survive and that get most of their food from the ocean

predator: an animal that hunts, kills, and eats other animals

prey: an animal hunted by a predator

reflects: bounces off, such as light bouncing off a mirror

sleuth: a group of bears

Note to readers: Some of these words may have more than one definition. The definitions above match how these words are used in this book.

CONTENTS

Polar bears are super!
How do their paws help them
swim fast and walk on ice?
Why do they roll in snow
or touch noses?

Why does their fur look white, and what color is it really? By the time you get to the end of this book, you'll know all about what makes polar bears amazing!

CHAPTER 1

MARINE BEARS

Polar bears are marine (say: muh-REEN) animals, which means they need to live near the ocean to survive in the wild.

They are the only marine bears.

Polar bears live in the Arctic, the area around the Earth's North Pole. The water is so cold there that a lot of the surface, or top, is frozen. Ice is no problem for polar bears, though!

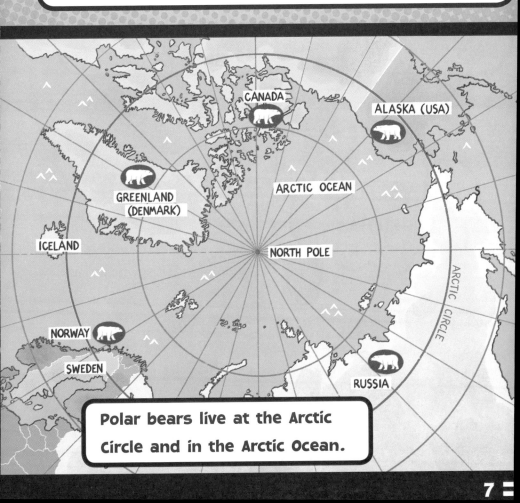

Polar bears live at the Arctic Circle and in the Arctic Ocean.

Polar bears are predators (say: PRED-uh-ters), which means they hunt and eat other animals. The animals that predators eat are called prey (say: PRAY). Polar bears mostly eat seals. Seals have a lot of blubber.

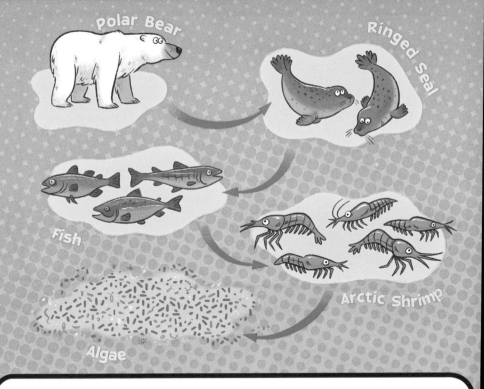

Polar Bear

Ringed Seal

Fish

Arctic Shrimp

Algae

Blubber is a special kind of fat that
helps marine animals store energy,
stay warm, and float more easily!
If a polar bear can't find seals
to eat, it will eat reindeer, rodents,
seaweed, and just about anything else!
Polar bears can survive without food
for up to 240 days.

Sometimes, if a polar bear is hungry, it will ask another polar bear to share its meal.
It asks by touching noses with the other polar bear!

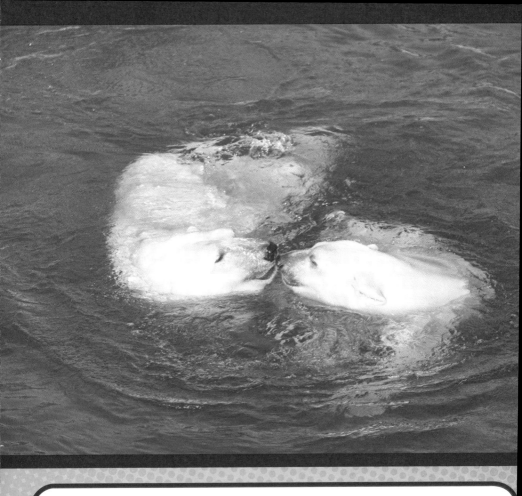

Polar bears also touch noses to greet each other.

While they spend a lot of time alone, when polar bears are in a group, they are called a sleuth (say: SLOOTH) of polar bears!

Polar bears are the largest carnivores (say: KAR-nuh-vores), or animals that eat meat, that live on land.

LIONS

Nearly nine feet long and up to **420** pounds

Even so, when they are born, polar bear cubs are very small at around twelve inches long. That is as long as a ruler, or an adult guinea pig!

Before cubs are born, their mother makes a snow den by digging a cave in the snow. Mothers usually give birth in the snow den, and often have twins!

Newborn cubs cannot see or hear. They stay in the warm den with their mother until they're about four months old.

In the winter, the temperature in the Arctic is often way below freezing. Luckily, polar bears have about four inches of blubber under their skin that helps them stay warm. Sometimes they have to dive into icy water to cool off!

The blubber keeps the bears from losing heat from their bodies. So little heat escapes that if you used a special video camera that "sees" only heat, polar bears would be almost invisible!

Polar bears have other cool abilities. Their huge paws help them walk on top of thin ice and deep snow.

Like snowshoes that humans wear, the big paws spread out the bear's weight and put less pressure on the snow or ice below.

Their claws can be two inches long!

The bottoms of their paws have another amazing feature. They have small, soft bumps that grip the ice.

What is pizza?

A polar bear's paw is about twelve inches in diameter—about the same size as a medium pizza.

Another fun fact about feet?
Polar bear paws have glands that
leave behind a scent that helps
polar bears find one another.
This is possible because polar bears
have an excellent sense of smell.
On land, they can smell a seal
from twenty miles away.

They can also smell a seal in the water, even when the seal is swimming under more than three feet of ice and snow.

That's not all! Polar bears can swim at speeds of about six miles per hour. That's the same speed as Olympic swimming champion Michael Phelps!

Polar bears have webbing between their toes, so their feet act like flippers to make them swim faster!

Their back legs help them change direction when they swim, similar to the rudder on a ship.

Polar bears can also run at speeds of up to twenty-five miles per hour on land. Most of the time, though, polar bears sit still at seal breathing holes, waiting for seals to appear.

Their nostrils close up underwater.

They have webbed feet.

In addition to blubber, thick fur helps polar bears stay warm.

Clean fur does the best job of keeping out the cold.

How does a polar bear keep its fur clean?

By rolling in snow!

It's like taking a snow bath!

A polar bear's top layer of fur is hollow, which means each hair has an open space in the middle of it. The hollow space inside the fur traps body heat and helps keep the polar bear warm!

Polar bear fur looks white, which makes them blend in with white snow when they hunt. If you looked under a microscope, you would see that up close their fur is clear, with no color at all. Objects look the color they do because of how light reflects, or bounces, off the object.

A rainbow contains all of the visible colors.

Sunlight looks white. When sunlight hits polar bear fur, the white light bounces around the hollow space inside each hair and then bounces back out again. The white light makes clear polar bear fur look white too.

Underneath the fur, polar bear skin is black. Something looks black when all the colors of sunlight are absorbed and none are reflected. This helps black objects absorb more heat from sunlight too.
The color of polar bear skin makes it easier for the bears to stay warm.

If you could be like a polar bear, would you like to stay so warm that you wouldn't ever need a jacket?

Would you want to have feet that work like snowshoes and flippers?

Polar bears are really neat, but what do you think is the most interesting thing about them? The choice is yours!

Turn the page to learn about how protecting the planet can help polar bears, too!

SAVE POLAR BEARS, SAVE THE WORLD

Unfortunately, the number of polar bears in the world is dropping, in part because Earth's climate is getting hotter. Climate is the average measurement of temperature, wind, rain, and snow in a place over time. The climate where polar bears live is getting warmer more quickly than at any other time in history. This is causing sea ice to melt.

Scientists believe that climate change is happening because of human activities, like burning fuel and cutting down trees, which increase the amount of carbon dioxide in Earth's atmosphere. Carbon dioxide traps heat and causes high temperatures.

You can help slow down climate change every day by saving energy. Turn off the lights when you leave a room, and ask your family to try walking instead of taking the car when you're not going very far. Plant a tree, if you can. By being thoughtful today, you can make the world a better place for polar bears—and humans!